Merry Christmas!
THINGS TO MAKE AND DO

Written by Robyn Supraner
Illustrated by Renzo Barto

Troll Associates

Library of Congress Cataloging in Publication Data

Supraner, Robyn.
    Merry Christmas.

    SUMMARY: Christmas projects for decorations, gifts,
and cards.
    1. Christmas decorations—Juvenile literature.
2. Handicraft—Juvenile literature. [1. Christmas
decorations. 2. Handicraft] I. Barto, Renzo.
II. Title.
TT900.C4S86   745.594'1   80-23884
ISBN 0-89375-422-6
ISBN 0-89375-423-4 (pbk.)

CONTENTS

Before you begin—

Read all the directions for your project.

Have everything you need ready.

Spread old newspapers on the table where you are working, when using paints and glue.

Leave enough time to clean up when you are finished.

Christmas is a time of joy and giving. Trimming the tree and exchanging presents with friends and family are special parts of this happy holiday. The ideas and projects on the following pages will make Christmas all the merrier! So get busy—and have fun!

SNOWMAN

Here's what you need:

Sheet of
white typing paper

Black, felt-tipped
marker

Glue

Scissors

Pencil

Piece of string
or colored yarn

Here's what you do:

1 Fold the sheet of paper in half. Fold it in half again... and again.

2 Open the paper and refold it, like a fan or an accordion.

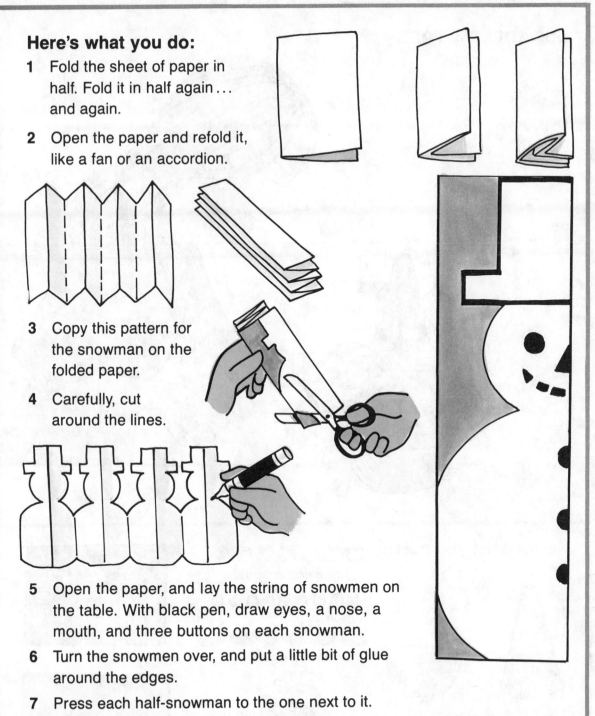

3 Copy this pattern for the snowman on the folded paper.

4 Carefully, cut around the lines.

5 Open the paper, and lay the string of snowmen on the table. With black pen, draw eyes, a nose, a mouth, and three buttons on each snowman.

6 Turn the snowmen over, and put a little bit of glue around the edges.

7 Press each half-snowman to the one next to it.

8 Before gluing the last two halves together, place the string or colored yarn in the seam. Glue the halves together over the string, to hold the string in place.

SUGARPLUM TREE

Here's what you need:

Tiny marshmallows

Gumdrops

Spearmint leaves

Styrofoam cone, large enough to fit into an empty 1-pound margarine container

Toothpicks

Colored yarn

Green foil

Red tissue paper

Here's what you do:

1 Place the plastic container on the red tissue paper. Gather the paper up over the cup, and tie the colored yarn around the paper.

2 Wrap the green foil around the cone and stand it in the plastic container.

3 Place a gumdrop, spearmint leaf, and a marshmallow on a toothpick. Stick the toothpick into the styrofoam tree.

4 Place as many toothpicks as you like all over the tree. Use the Sugarplum Tree as a centerpiece. Eat the candy for dessert.

SLED

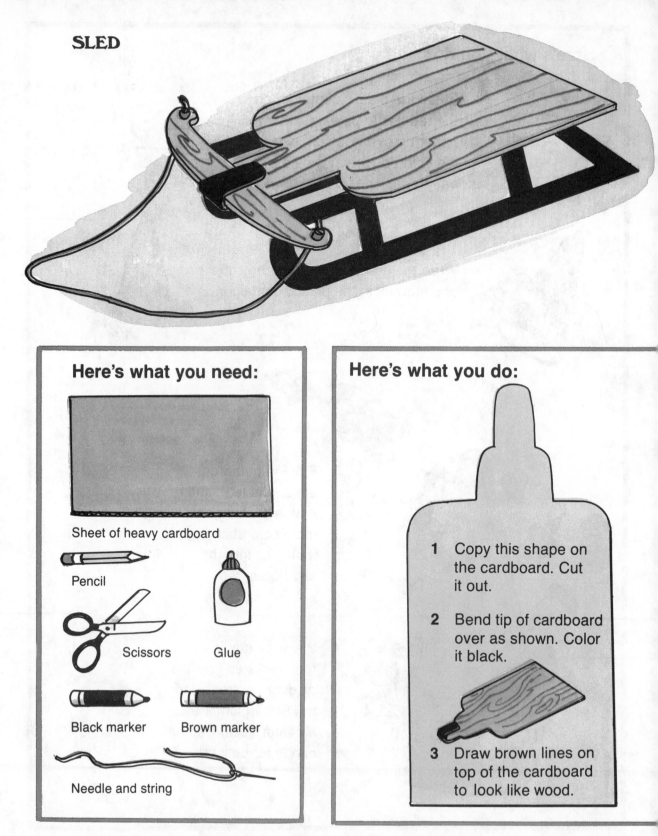

Here's what you need:

Sheet of heavy cardboard

Pencil

Scissors

Glue

Black marker

Brown marker

Needle and string

Here's what you do:

1   Copy this shape on the cardboard. Cut it out.

2   Bend tip of cardboard over as shown. Color it black.

3   Draw brown lines on top of the cardboard to look like wood.

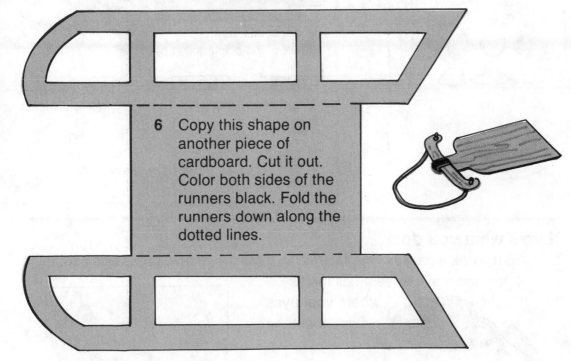

4 Copy this shape for the sled's handle, and cut it out. Add brown markings to look like wood. Make two small holes, one at each end of the handle.

5 Thread string through the holes, and knot each end. Place the handle under the black tip on the other piece of cardboard. Glue the handle in place where the black tip touches it.

6 Copy this shape on another piece of cardboard. Cut it out. Color both sides of the runners black. Fold the runners down along the dotted lines.

7 Glue the parts of the sled together.

Hang the sled by its string from your Christmas tree. Or make more than one sled. Use them for place cards at Christmas dinner.

SANTA CLAUS MASK

Here's what you need:

Cotton

Sheet of oak tag
Sheet of red construction paper

Scissors

Black and red markers

2 Loose-leaf reinforcements

Glue   String or heavy yarn

Here's what you do:

1 Hold the oak tag up to your face. With a marker, gently press against the oak tag and make three small marks where your eyes and mouth are.

2 Cut two circles for the eyes. Cut a rectangle for the mouth. Cut away areas on the sides to form the ears. Make a small hole in each ear.

3 Make Santa's hat from red construction paper. Use the shape shown here.

4 Glue the hat to the oak tag.

5 Draw tassle line on hat with black marker.

6 Using red marker, give Santa a round, cherry nose, two rosy cheeks, and a red bottom lip.

7 Cut a half-circle under nose.

8 Trim his hat with a strip of cotton. Use a cotton ball for the tip of his tassle. Give him a cotton beard and a twirly mustache. Give him two cotton eyebrows.

9 Glue everything in place.

10 Stick a loose-leaf reinforcement behind each ear around the holes.

11 Tie two pieces of yarn or string through the holes.

CHRISTMAS BALLS

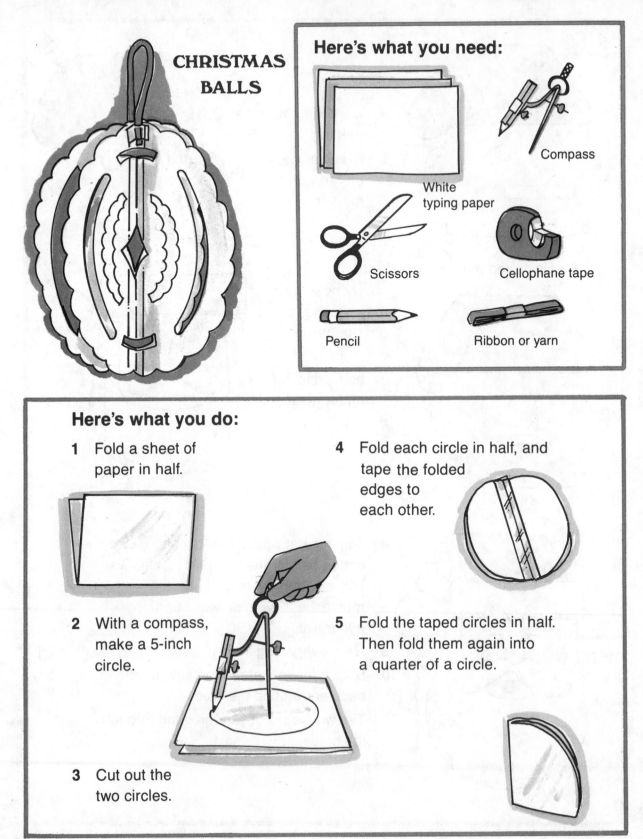

Here's what you need:

White typing paper

Compass

Scissors

Cellophane tape

Pencil

Ribbon or yarn

Here's what you do:

1 Fold a sheet of paper in half.

2 With a compass, make a 5-inch circle.

3 Cut out the two circles.

4 Fold each circle in half, and tape the folded edges to each other.

5 Fold the taped circles in half. Then fold them again into a quarter of a circle.

6 Draw a design on the folded circle. Copy this one, or make one of your own.

7 With your scissors, carefully cut out the design.

8 Take an 8-inch piece of ribbon or yarn, and place a strip of cellophane tape at each end.

9 Open the folded circles to make two complete circles. Tape the ribbon to the circles to form a loop for hanging the ornament. Hang it from a window shade. Or hang it from a lamp. Or hang it from a gift-wrapped box to make an extra pretty package.

Here's what you need:

White typing paper

Compass

Pencil

Scissors

Glue

SNOWFLAKES

Here's what you do:

1 With a compass, draw the biggest circle you can on a sheet of typing paper.

2 Cut out the circle, and fold it in half.

3 Fold the half into thirds. Make sharp creases along the folds.

4 Draw a pretty design like the ones on this page, or make one of your own.

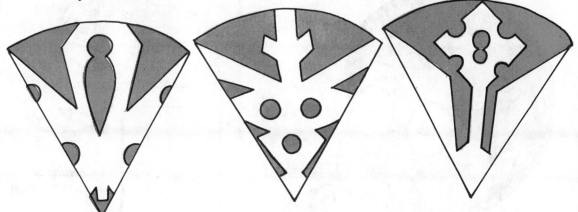

5 Carefully cut out the design.

6 Now, cut some circles and triangles along the two straight edges. Cut big ones and small ones. (*Note:* Cut just a few shapes at first. When you have more experience, you can add more cuts. The more cuts you make, the lacier your snowflake will be.)

7 Open the snowflake very slowly. Be careful not to tear it.

Snowflakes make pretty place mats. Glue a big snowflake and a smaller one to a sheet of green or red construction paper. Make a place mat for each member of your family. Use them at breakfast on Christmas morning!

Or attach a flurry of snowflakes to your window. Stick them on with cellophane tape. You can also glue a few snowflakes to red wrapping paper, and wrap up a present for someone you love!

CANDY BASKETS

Here's what you need:

Cardboard egg carton

Crayons or colored markers

Sheet of typing paper

Ribbon or yarn

Pencil

Scissors

Glue

Mug

Here's what you do:

1 From a cardboard egg carton, cut one of the cups that hold the eggs.

2 Cut a pretty edge around the top of the cup.

18

3 Poke a small hole on either side of the cup.

4 Thread a piece of ribbon or yarn through the holes. Knot it in place.

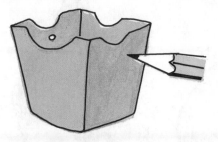

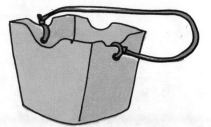

(*Note:* If you like, use a pipe cleaner for the basket's handle, instead. Bend the ends to hold it in place.)

5 On a sheet of typing paper, trace around a cup or mug.

6 With a crayon or marker, draw a thick scalloped edge around the circle.

7 Cut out the circle, and draw the scalloped edge on the other side of it.

8 Put a dab of glue in the bottom of the cup.

9 Press the circle inside the cup. Hold it in place until the glue is dry.

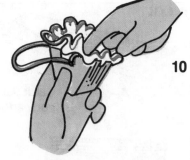

10 Fill the basket with jelly beans or Christmas candy. Hang it from a Christmas tree or give it to a friend.

EGG-CARTON ORNAMENTS

Here's what you need:

Colored construction paper

Cardboard egg carton

Pipe cleaners

Glue

Scissors

Here's what you do:

1 From a cardboard egg carton, cut two of the tall crowns that separate the eggs.

2 Cut the edges straight, so the crowns will fit together.

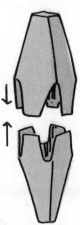

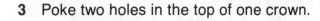

3 Poke two holes in the top of one crown.

4 Bend a pipe cleaner gently in half. Push the ends of the pipe cleaner through the holes. Bend each end sharply, so it looks like a capital L.

5 Put a thin line of glue around the edge of one crown. Press both crowns together. Hold them in place until the glue is dry.

6 Cut pretty designs from colored construction paper. Cut triangles, circles, and flower shapes. Cut holly leaves and small red berries. Glue your designs to the ornament, and hang it on the tree.

HOLLY WREATH

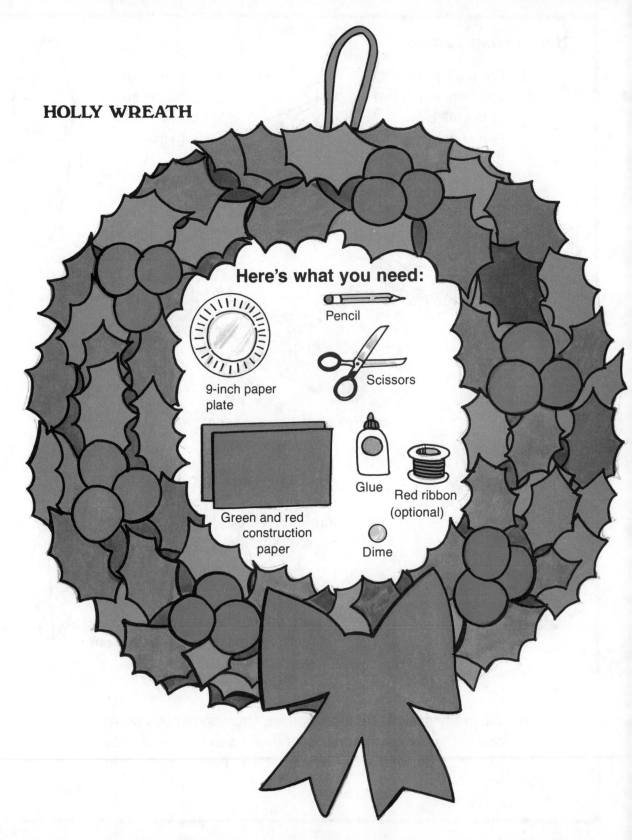

Here's what you need:

9-inch paper plate

Pencil

Scissors

Green and red construction paper

Glue

Red ribbon (optional)

Dime

Here's what you do:

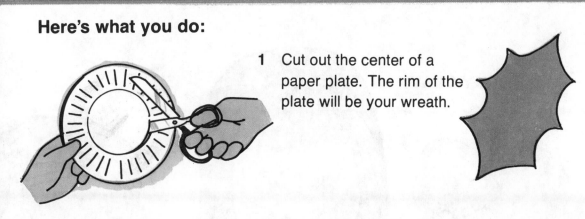

1   Cut out the center of a paper plate. The rim of the plate will be your wreath.

2   On green construction paper, copy this holly-leaf pattern. Trace as many leaves as you can fit on the paper. Carefully cut them out. Your holly leaves should have sharp points.

3   Glue the leaves to the plate. Overlap them to completely cover the plate. Make more leaves, if you need them.

4   From red construction paper, make small berries by tracing around a dime.

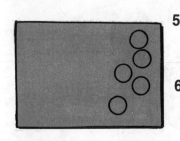

5   Cut out the berries.

6   Glue them, in bunches of three, to the wreath.

7   Add a bow made of red paper. Or use ribbon—a red ribbon bow looks especially nice!

8   Hang your wreath in a window, or use it to decorate a wall or door.

KOOKY CLAY

Here's what you need:

1 Cup flour

¼ Cup salt

⅓ Cup water

Mixing bowl

Wooden spoon

Plastic bags

Here's what you do:

1 Put the flour, salt, and water in a bowl.

2 Mix well with a wooden spoon. When it is well mixed, press the clay between your fingers to get out any lumps. (*Note:* If the clay feels dry and crumbly, add a few drops of water. If it feels too mushy, add a bit of flour.)

3 Store the clay in a plastic bag. It will keep for a long time in the refrigerator, but let it warm to room temperature, when you are ready to use it.

Kooky Clay is good for making tree ornaments and small figures. It can be painted with any water-base paint. If you like, you can give the clay a nice shine by brushing a coat of clear nail polish over the paint.

PAINTED TREE ORNAMENTS

Here are
some figures
you may
want to try.

Here's what you need:

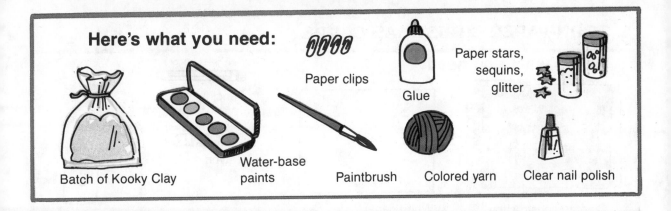

Batch of Kooky Clay

Water-base paints

Paper clips

Paintbrush

Glue

Colored yarn

Paper stars, sequins, glitter

Clear nail polish

Here's what you do:

1 Make simple figures with Kooky Clay. Keep the figures small, so they will dry evenly. (*Note:* If you like, roll out the clay on wax paper. Use cookie cutters to make the shapes you want.)

2 While the ornaments are still soft, press a paper clip into the top of each one. Make sure the top of the clip sticks out over the top of the figure.

3 Let the figures dry for 2 or 3 days.

4 Color them with paint. When they are dry, brush them with a coat of clear nail polish. Decorate them with paper stars, sequins, glitter, or anything else you can think of.

5 String colored yarn through the paper-clip loops, and hang the ornaments from the Christmas tree.

TORN-PAPER CHRISTMAS CARDS

Here's what you need:

Colored construction paper

White paper

Pencil

Crayon

Glue

Here's what you do:

1   Fold a sheet of construction paper in half to make the card.

2   Plan a simple design. A flower is a good way to begin. Sketch your

flower on a piece of paper. A poinsettia is a good flower for the Christmas season.

3   From colored paper, tear the shapes you will need to complete the design. Use crayon to fill in any details.

4   Glue the shapes into place on your card.

Try making one of the cards on these two pages. Or think up an idea of your own.

This is an idea for a zig-zag, fold-out card.

RIBBON CHRISTMAS CARDS

Here's what you need:

Colored construction paper

Shiny paper ribbon

Scissors   Glue

Here's what you do:

1 Fold a sheet of construction paper in half. Hold it so it opens from the side or the bottom.

2 Plan a simple design. For a Christmas tree: Cut six pieces of green ribbon. Cut the ribbon into three different sizes, each a bit longer than the others. Cut two pieces of each size. Glue the pieces of ribbon to the construction paper. Glue them in the shape of a tree. Cut a star and a tree trunk from gold ribbon. Glue them in place. Open the card, and write a message inside.

3 For a holly wreath: Cut about 25 small triangles from green ribbon. Glue them to the card in the shape of a wreath. Cut 12 little circles from red ribbon. These are the berries. Glue them on the wreath. Make a bow with gold ribbon. Glue it to the bottom of the wreath.

4 For bells:

Draw two bell shapes on a piece of construction paper. Glue four strips of ribbon over each bell shape, about ⅛ inch apart. When the glue is dry, cut out each bell, and glue it to your Christmas card. Cut out two small circles from another piece of ribbon and glue in place for bell clappers. Fold a length of ribbon and glue to the tops of the bells.

CHRISTMAS STOCKING

Here's what you need:

Straight pins

Heavy paper

Colored yarn

Piece of red felt, twice
as big as the stocking
you're planning to make

Glue

Scissors

Pencil

Crayon

Decorations: yarn, sequins, scraps of colored felt, rickrack, embroidery thread and needle,
or anything else you would like

Here's what you do:

1 Draw a pattern for the stocking on a piece of heavy paper.

2 Cut out the pattern. Pin it to a piece of red felt that has been folded in half.

3 Carefully cut around the pattern. You will have two stocking-shaped pieces of felt.

4 Decorate the pieces any way you like. Cut out the letters of your name from scraps of felt or other material. Glue them to the stocking. Decorate the stocking—you can embroider flower designs with a needle and thread, or glue on a row of sequins, or make a Santa Claus.

5 After you have decorated both sides, use a piece of heavy yarn to make a handle. Glue it to the wrong side of one of the stocking pieces. Put a ribbon of glue along the edges of that side, but don't put any glue across the top edge. Press the two stocking pieces together.

For extra strength, stitch around the edge of the stocking.

STOCKING STUFFERS

Here's what you need:

Cardboard egg carton

Scissors

Glue

Decorations: sequins, stars, glitter

Colored ribbon or heavy yarn

Old magazines

Pencil

Here's what you do:

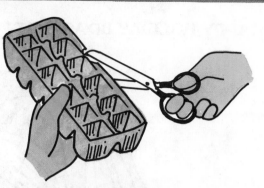

1 Cut two cups from a cardboard egg carton.

2 Cut the edges straight.

3 Decorate the cups with colored paper or silver stars. Sprinkle them with glitter. Sparkle them with sequins. Splash them with paint.

Use pictures cut from magazines. Use your imagination!

4 Put a jingle bell inside.

Chocolate kisses or tiny jelly beans make good surprises too. How about a secret message, rolled up and tucked inside?

5 Tie the cups together with ribbon or yarn.

WHY IS A CAT IN the dESERT LIkE CHRISTMAS?

THEY BOTH HAVE SANDY CLAWS.

35

HAPPY HOLIDAY BRACELET

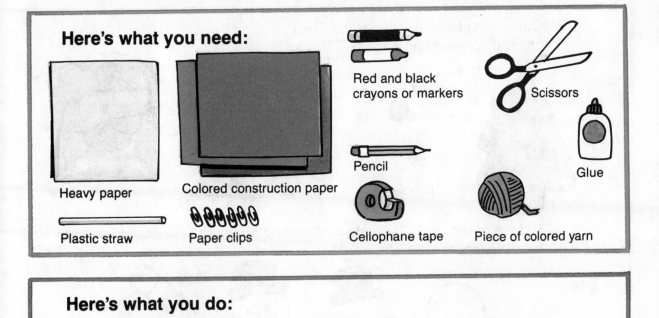

Here's what you need:

Red and black crayons or markers

Scissors

Pencil

Glue

Heavy paper

Colored construction paper

Plastic straw

Paper clips

Cellophane tape

Piece of colored yarn

Here's what you do:

1   On a piece of heavy paper, draw patterns for any of these shapes.
Or use one of your own.

2 Cut out the patterns, and trace them on colored construction paper.

Make a green tree. Decorate it with snips of colored paper. Add some black lines with your crayon.

Make a white snowman. Draw black eyes, nose, and mouth. Give him some buttons.

Make a red bell. If you like, glue the bell to a piece of silver foil. Cut away the extra foil.

Make a white candy cane. Draw red stripes on it.

Make a green wreath. Decorate it with red paper berries and a bow.

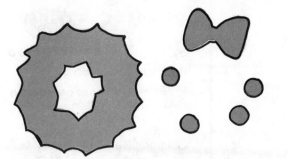 

3 Turn over each shape and tape a paper clip to it.

4 Cut the straw in half. Cut each half into six pieces. You will have twelve pieces.

5 String the Christmas tree on a piece of yarn about 10 inches long. Pull the yarn through the paper-clip loop.

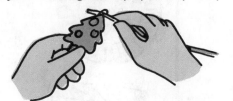

6 String two pieces of the straw.

7 Next, string the snowman. Then, two more pieces of straw.

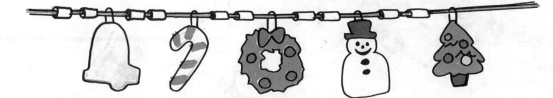

Continue stringing until you have used all the shapes and ten pieces of straw.

8 Tie the ends of the yarn into a bow.

9 If the bracelet is too small, add the extra pieces of straw. If the bracelet is too big, take some away. If necessary, snip off a bit of yarn. Now your bracelet is ready to wear or to give as a gift.

(Note: To make your bracelet even prettier, cut two of each shape. Glue them, back to back, to cover the paper clip. Decorate only one side.)

PINE-CONE CHRISTMAS TREE

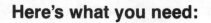

Here's what you need:

Pine cone

Beads
Sequins
Red hots
Dragees
Silver foil

Gold or silver star

Glue

Talcum powder

Tweezer

Cotton

Silver doily or red paper plate

Here's what you do:

1 Decorate the pine cone. Use beads, sequins, red hots, or silver dragees. If you like, use them all. Glue them in place.
(*Note:* Use a tweezer—it will make the job easier.)

2 Weave a few strands of silver foil through the petals.

3 Glue a bright, shiny star on the top.

4 Put a mound of snowy, white cotton on a silver doily or a red paper plate.

5 Place the pine cone on the cotton. Sprinkle it lightly with talcum powder.

6 Stand it on a shelf or small table for everyone to admire!

Here's what you need:

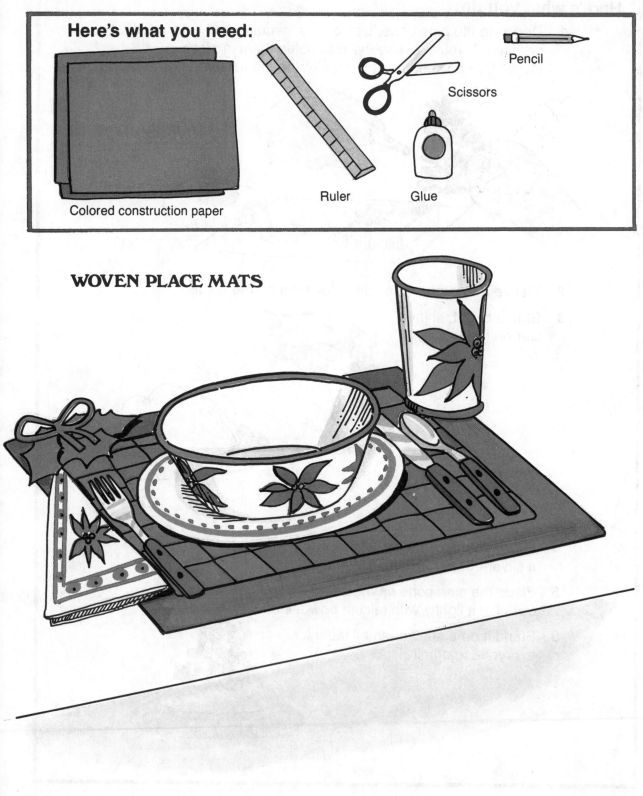

Colored construction paper

Ruler

Scissors

Glue

Pencil

WOVEN PLACE MATS

Here's what you do:

1 On a sheet of red construction paper, draw 9 lines that are 1¼ inches apart. Keep the lines 1½ inches from the sides of the paper and 1 inch from the top and bottom. Keep the lines as straight as possible.

2 Make 9 slits in the paper along the 9 lines.

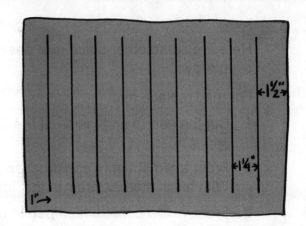

3 Cut 7, 1³⁄₁₆ x 10-inch strips of green construction paper.

4 Weave the green strips in and out of the place mat. Glue down the ends. Turn the mat over and glue down any loose ends.

5 Cut a 1½-inch frame from a second sheet of construction paper.

6 Put a ribbon of glue around the border of the mat, and place the frame over it.

7 Decorate the mat with green holly leaves and a red bow cut from colored paper. Make as many place mats as you need for your party.

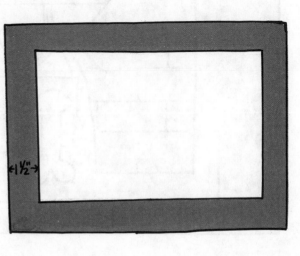

Here are some other place-mat designs you can use. Or make some of your own.

For the fireplace mat:

1 Cut the hearth and inside of the fireplace out of purple construction paper.

2 From a red sheet of construction paper, cut out the fireplace shape. With black marker, draw in the lines of the bricks.

3 From yellow construction paper, cut out andirons and the flames.

4 From brown construction paper, cut out a strip for the mantel and the log.

5 Cut out two stockings from any colors you like.

6 Glue everything in place.

7 You can add your guests' names to the stockings to show everyone where to sit at the table.

For the candle:

1 Cut a wide band of green construction paper, and glue it across a sheet of red construction paper.

2 Cut a circle from yellow construction paper and a flame from red paper.

3 From white paper, cut a candle shape. From orange paper, cut a candle holder.

4 Glue all pieces in place.

WINTER WONDERLAND

Here's what you need:

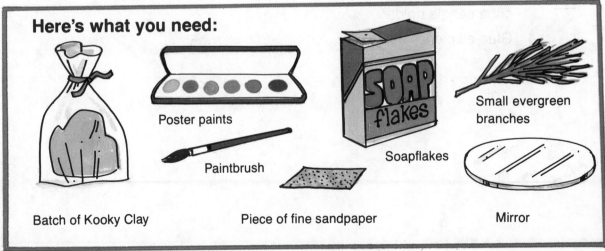

Poster paints

Paintbrush

Batch of Kooky Clay

Piece of fine sandpaper

SOAP flakes

Soapflakes

Small evergreen branches

Mirror

Here's what you do:

1. Make a snowman with Kooky Clay. Make boys and girls, a dog, and a log. Keep the figures simple. Make them small so they will dry evenly.

2. Put the figures where they will be out of the way. Let them dry for 2 or 3 days.

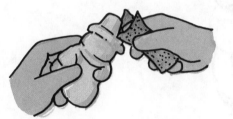

3. Gently smooth any rough spots with sandpaper.

4. Color the figures with poster paint. If you like, add scarfs and kerchiefs made from scraps of material.

5. Arrange the figures on a mirror.

6. Add some trees or bushes made from evergreen branches. Hold the branches in place with clay.

7. Sprinkle soapflakes on the mirror and trees. The soapflakes look like snowflakes. The mirror looks like ice!

8. Think of other things to add to your winter wonderland. How about a broom for the snowman? Or a pile of snowballs for a snow fight? Make a small sled so the children can go for a ride.